Gershwin *for* Students

7 Graded Arrangements for Late Elementary Pianists
Arranged by
Carol Matz

American composer George Gershwin (1898–1937) and his brother, lyricist Ira Gershwin (1896–1983), created some of the most imaginative and enduring American music. George Gershwin combined elements of jazz with traditional symphonic formats in his most famous compositions *Rhapsody in Blue, Concerto in F, An American in Paris,* as well as the folk opera *Porgy and Bess.* In addition, the two brothers collaborated to write numerous popular songs that have been recorded over the years by countless singers and jazz instrumentalists.

Gershwin for Students, Book 1, is arranged at the late-elementary level. Key signatures are limited to no more than one sharp or flat, and the pieces appear in approximate order of difficulty. The arrangements are carefully graded for students, while still retaining the flavor and feel of the original Gershwin compositions.

Produced by
Alfred Music Publishing Co., Inc.
P.O. Box 10003
Van Nuys, CA 91410-0003
alfred.com

Printed in USA.

ISBN-10: 0-7390-7957-3
ISBN-13: 978-0-7390-7957-7

SUMMERTIME

(from *Porgy and Bess*)

Music and Lyrics by George Gershwin,
Du Bose and Dorothy Heyward and Ira Gershwin
Arranged by Carol Matz

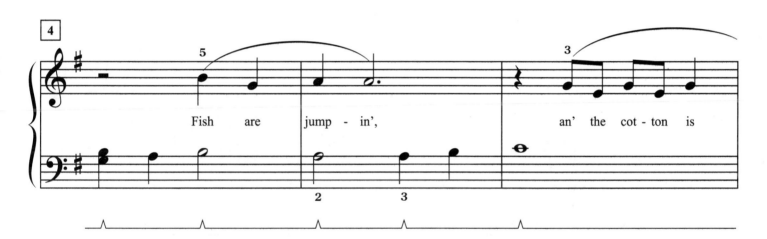

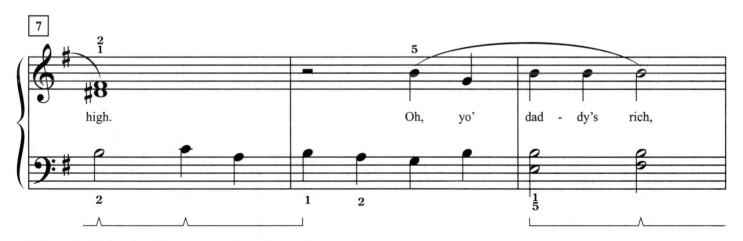

* Play all eighth notes with an uneven, long-short pattern.

SWANEE

Words by Irving Caesar
Music by George Gershwin
Arranged by Carol Matz

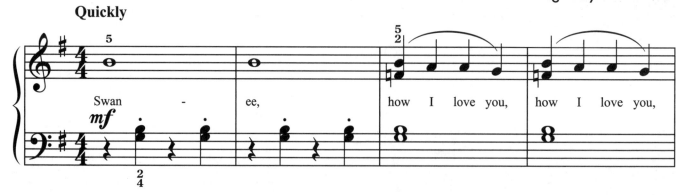

Swan - ee, how I love you, how I love you,

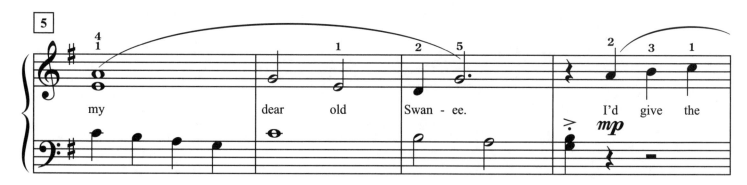

my dear old Swan - ee. I'd give the

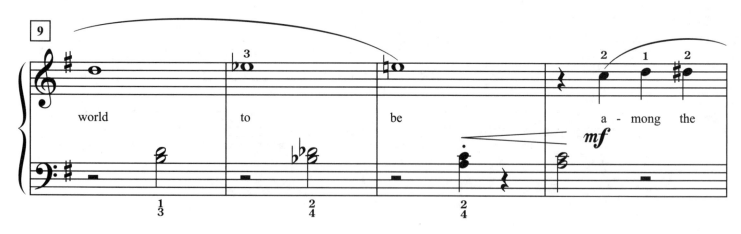

world to be a - mong the

folks in D - I - X - I - E - ven now my

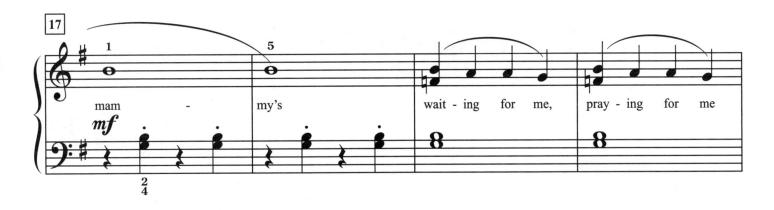

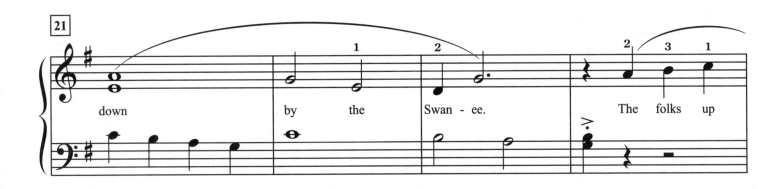

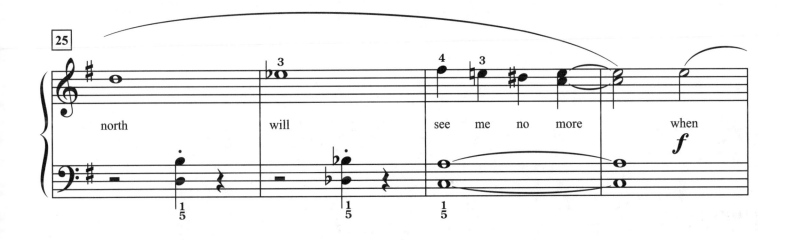

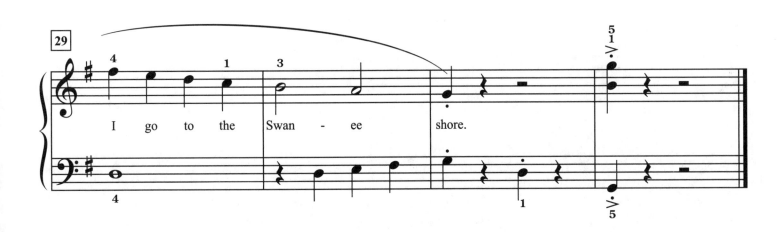

THREE-QUARTER BLUES

By George Gershwin
Arranged by Carol Matz

Moderately

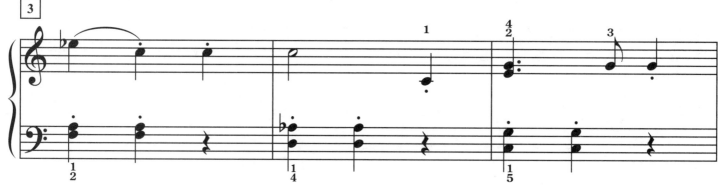

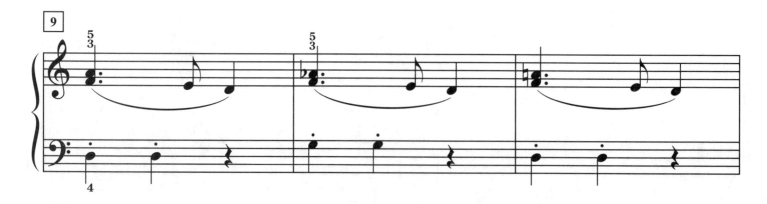

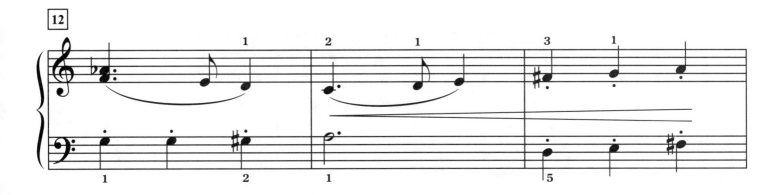

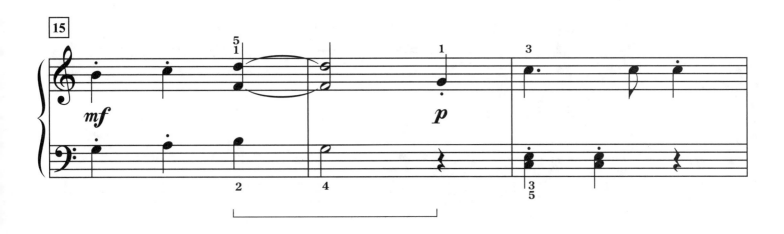

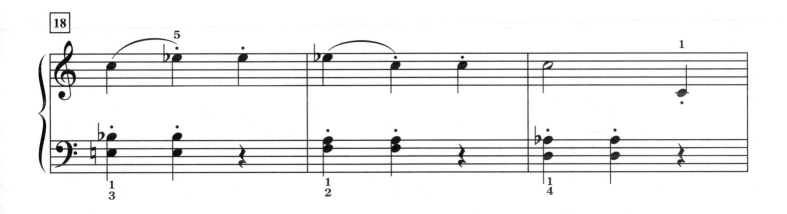

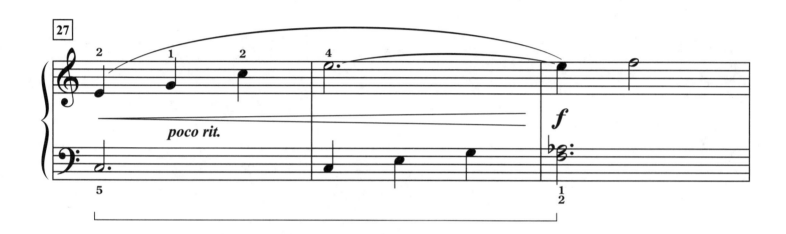

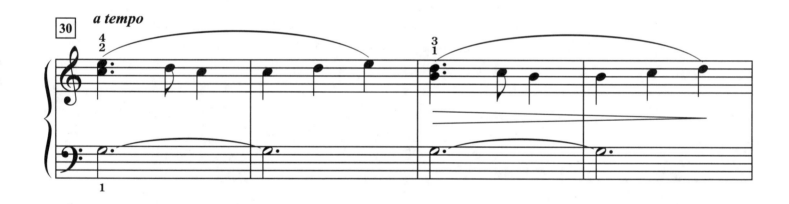

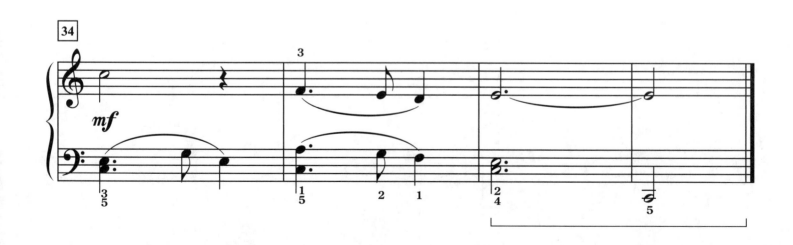

A FOGGY DAY
(In London Town)

Music and Lyrics by
George Gershwin and Ira Gershwin
Arranged by Carol Matz

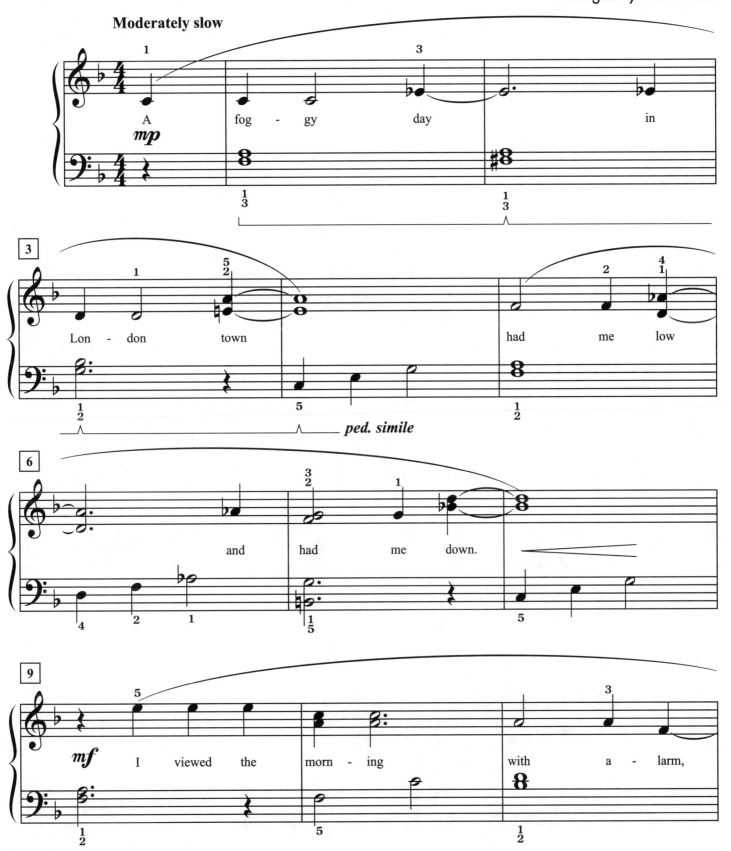

12 the Brit - ish Mu - se - um had

15 lost its charm. *mp* How long, I won -

18 dered, could this thing last? But the

ped. simile

21 age of mir - a - cles had - n't passed,

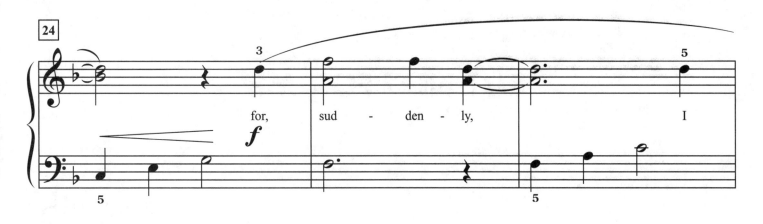

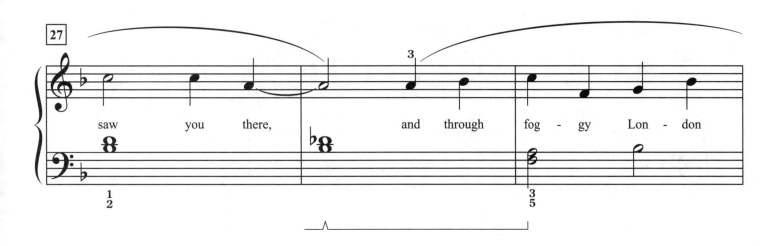

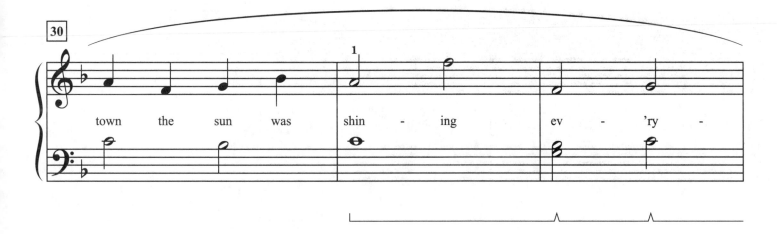

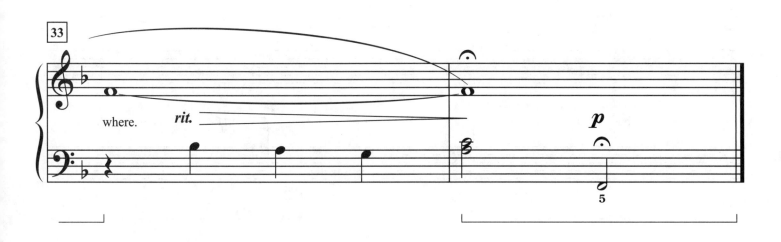

BUT NOT FOR ME

Music and Lyrics by
George Gershwin and Ira Gershwin
Arranged by Carol Matz

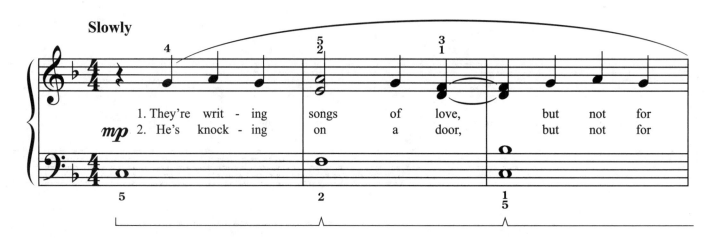

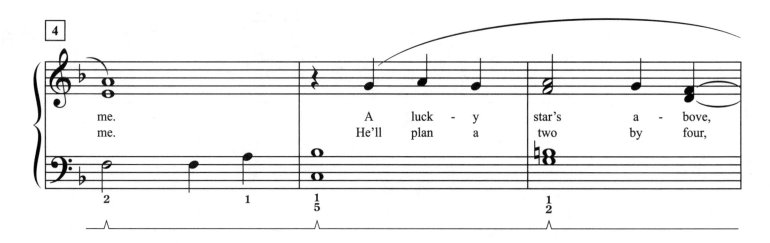

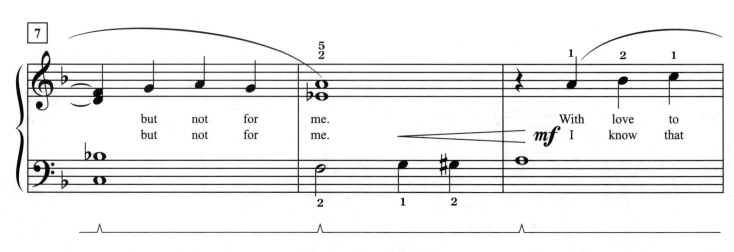

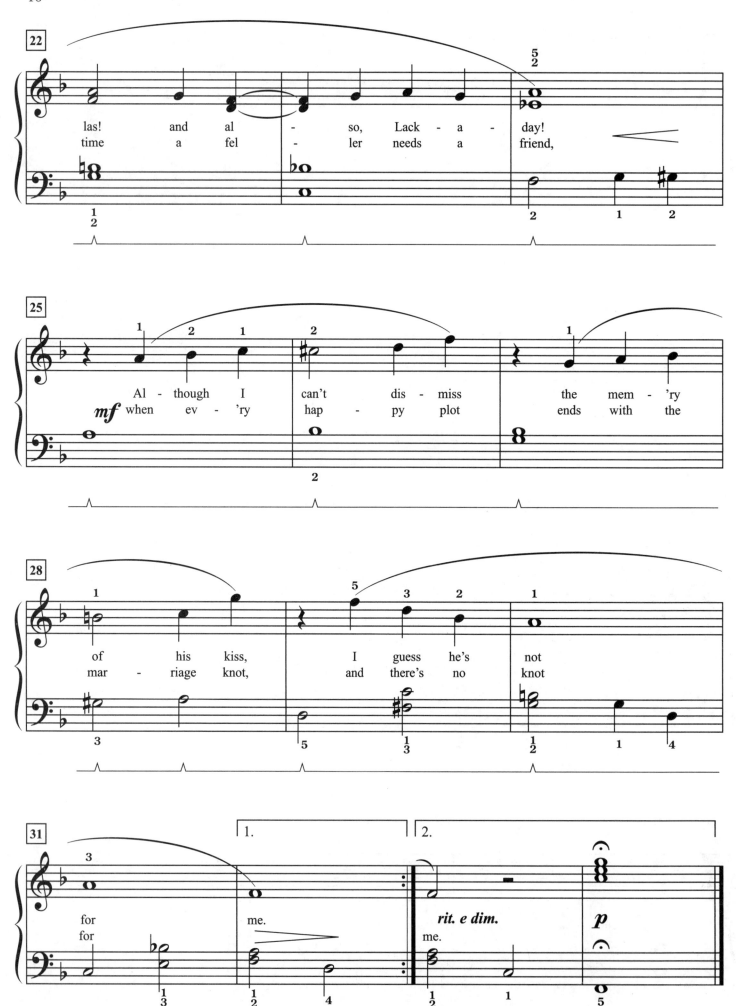

las! and al - so, Lack - a - day!
time a fel - ler needs a friend,

Al - though I can't dis - miss the mem - 'ry
when ev - 'ry hap - py plot ends with the

of his kiss, I guess he's not
mar - riage knot, and there's no knot

for me.
for me.

rit. e dim.

'S WONDERFUL

Music and Lyrics by
George Gershwin and Ira Gershwin
Arranged by Carol Matz

Moderately fast

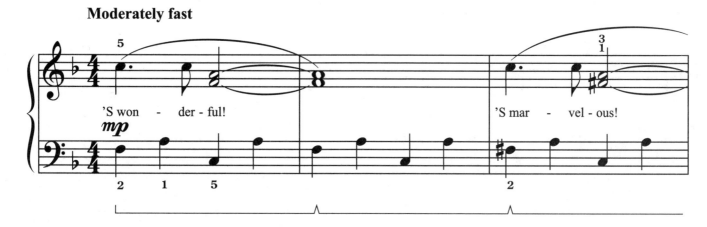

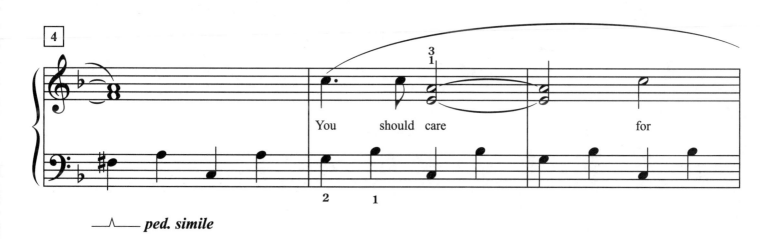

'S par - a - dise!

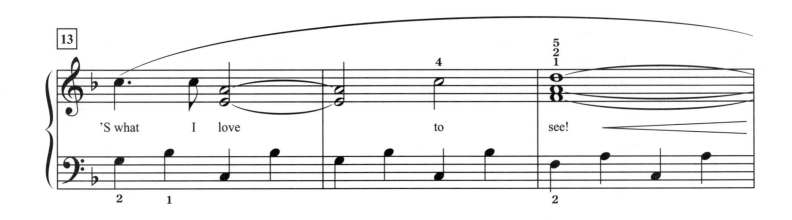

'S what   I   love   to   see!

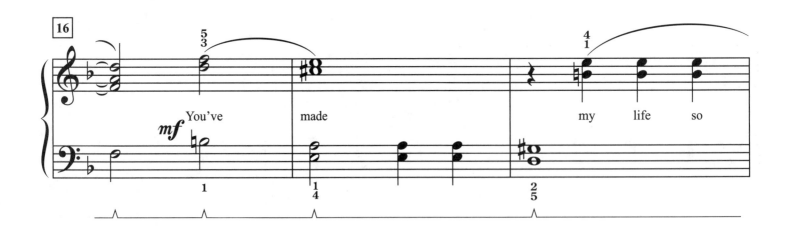

You've   made   my   life   so

mf

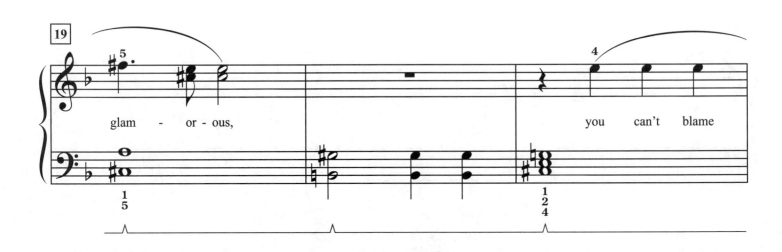

glam - or - ous,   you   can't   blame

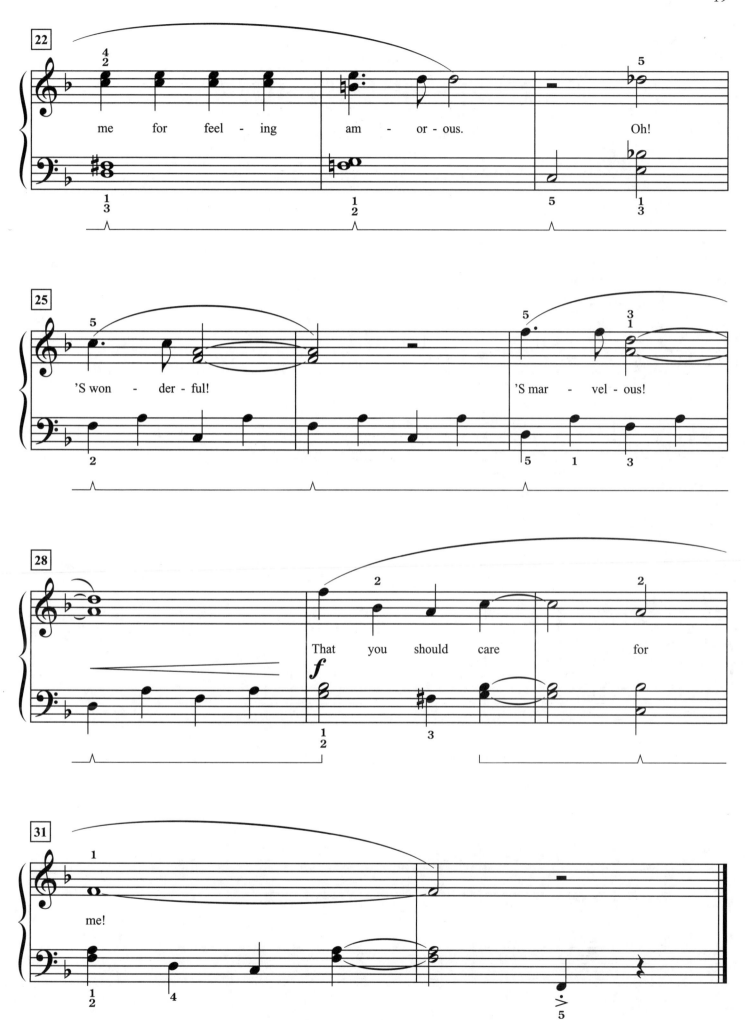

RHAPSODY IN BLUE

(Selected Themes)

Music by George Gershwin
Arranged by Carol Matz

Moderately

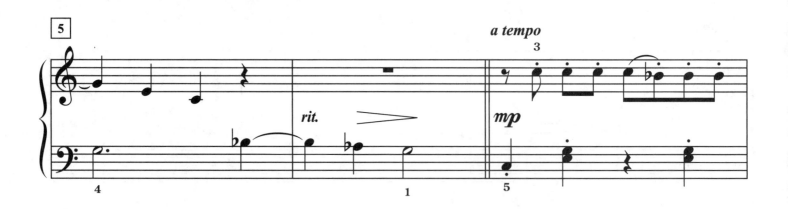

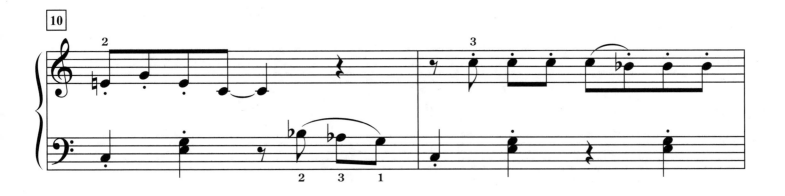

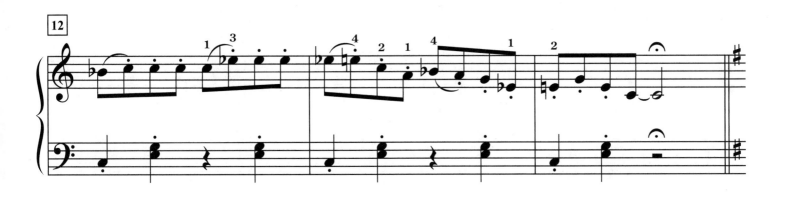

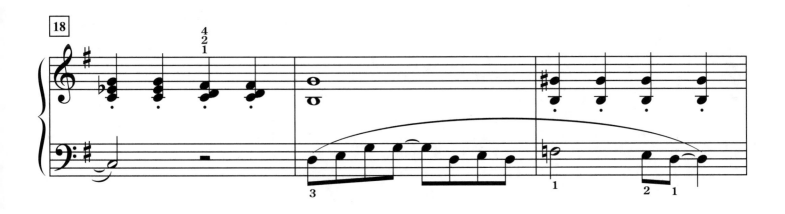

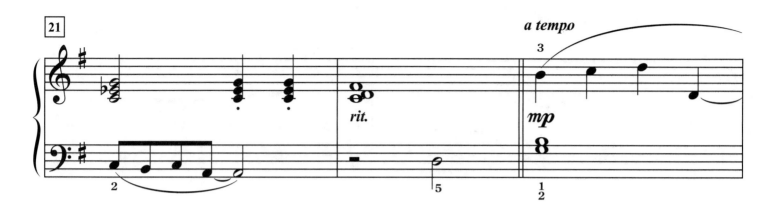

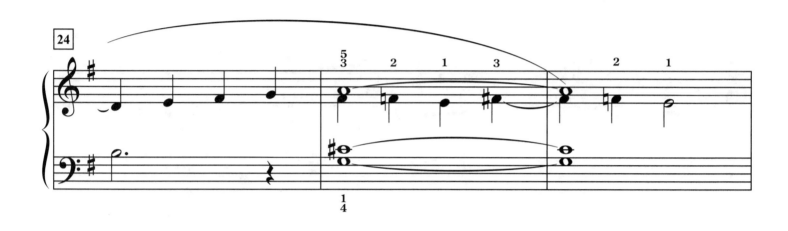

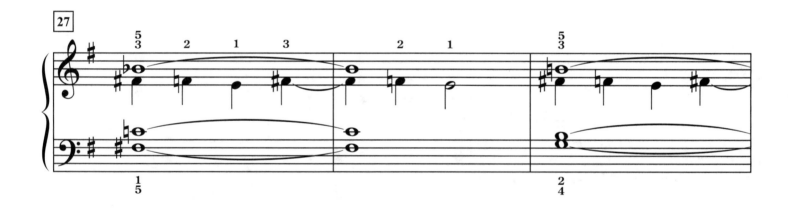

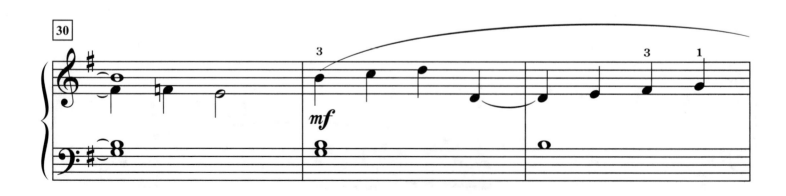

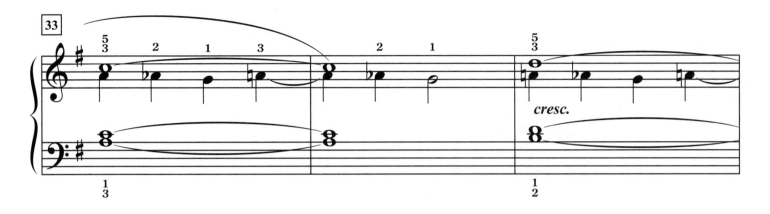

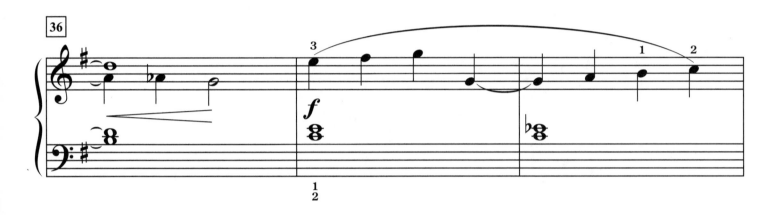

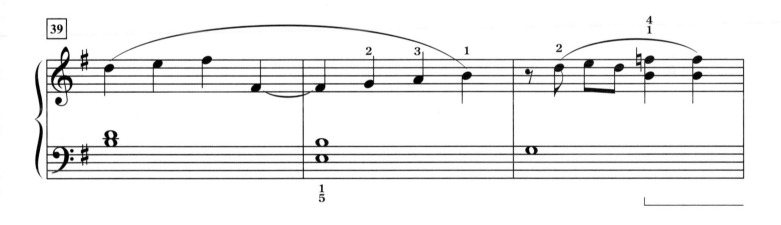

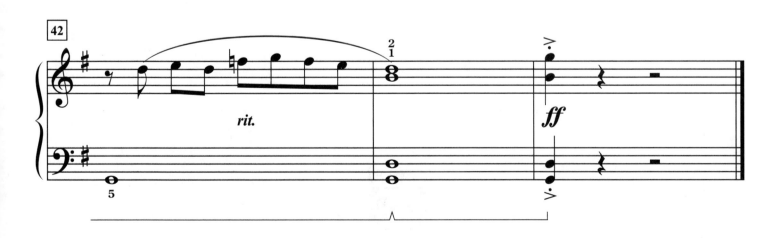